POWERHOUSE DIALING

How to Double your Income by Becoming a Phone Specialist

BY ANDY HERRINGTON

ISBN-13: 978-0-9920326-0-9

Published By:
Powerhouse Coaching Publications
Whitby, Ontario, Canada

Dedication:

To my Wife and Kids

CONTENTS

ACKNOWLEDGEMENTS:

"Behind every great man is a woman rolling her eyes"
  ~~ Jim Carrey

The very best part of my life is my personal life. My wife Cara is the most supportive person on the planet, the love of my life and everything I could ever have asked for and more. My two wonderful children Morgan and Sam are the light of my life and constantly pushing me to become better. I can't wait to see what you become. My close friends are few and far between, by choice, but Colin Cates, Graham Robertson and Phil Hayden you guys have truly made a difference in my life and I want to Thank you.

In business, I have had the opportunity to learn from and work with some of the very best people in the world. To anyone who I booked an appointment for, and you brought me back a Cheque… Thank You. As a Coach I love each and every one of my clients Thank you all for allowing me to do what I absolutely love to do.

Over the years I have had a slew of people who have influenced me and made me think, act and be the way I am. The people with the biggest influence that I would like to thank are: Zig Ziglar, Bob Fitzgerald, Matt Ferry, and Jim Rohn.

CHAPTER ONE

Introduction

Before you Act, LISTEN.
Before you React, THINK.
Before you Spend, EARN.
Before you Criticize, WAIT.
Before you Pray, FORGIVE.
Before you Quit, TRY.
~~~~ Ernest Hemingway

Everyone has their own specialty and Real Estate salespeople are no different. We all know that there are listing specialists, Farm specialists, Commercial Specialists and many more. Many Realtors struggle to figure out their niche, and I certainly was one of those. I struggled to determine what my specialty was during the first 4 years that I had my license. I think the main reason was because it just seemed like the thing I did best was not one of the "approved" specialties in Real Estate.

I never had any issues with picking up a phone and dialing, and I didn't have a problem talking to people either, however early on, I didn't have clue on what to say. Then even when I did book an appointment I would struggle at the in person portion of the business. The worst part of this was that there didn't seem to be a place for someone whose specialty was being on the phone.

Today some years later I realize that this specialty is not only desirable and wanted but also exceptionally rare to find. Almost every team I have been a part of or have coached over the last 4 years has wanted to implement a Phone Specialist Department. Sadly each of them has struggled to find the right people, and figure out how to build and run this department.

Shockingly most top producers do not enjoy the Phone aspect of Real Estate. Most referring to it as a necessary evil of the business, like print advertising. Top Producers are always looking to add people who can work the phones;

they are always worth their weight in gold. This means that if your specialty is working the phones, you can become a vital and important piece of a successful Real Estate Team and never have to do the parts of the job that you don't like.

Even more important than that, if you can add the aspect of being good on the phones to your own business, your success will only be restricted by your own boundaries.

This book will be a description of how to be, create or find a successful Phone Specialist. It can be used to help train a person, or help a fellow phone specialist feel less alone. I will tell my stories and share the tips I have learned during the over 350,000 phone calls and over 2100 transactions, plus the stories and knowledge I have gained from coaching Top Producing Real Estate Agents and Teams from all across Canada. This book will serve as a manual for the elusive and rewarding Inside Sales Career.

If used properly and implemented in a solid way the tools included in this book will help you to double your income or more. This is really that important to the long-term success of any Real Estate organization.

CHAPTER TWO
Phone Specialist

**To become the Superstar you wish to be, find your
Desired Expertise and Focus on it.**
  ~~ Andy Herrington

Many people in Real Estate have never heard of it, and even those that have call it by many different names. Inside Sales, Phone Sales, Lead Conversion Department, Telemarketers and more. These names are all correct. A phone specialist is all of those things. I have had many job titles over the years, but I call myself a Phone Specialist. I am truly great at dialing and talking to people on the phone and getting them to do what I need or require them to do.

I have always described the job of a phone specialist as taking $5000 dollar cheques and handing them off to someone and saying, "hey don't forget to give me my 500 bucks". The sad truth is you will spend just as much time watching the person roll that cheque up into a ball and throw it in the garbage as you will cashing the smaller cheques they return to you. This career is one the most rewarding and frustrating I have ever held.

The basic job description of a phone specialist is you are in charge of taking the leads, calling them, talking to the client, building rapport and getting them to meet face to face with an agent. But the job is a whole lot more complex than that. Phone specialists are the first impression for the organization, they are the first to build rapport with the clients and they are the main source of follow up for the business. They spend their day dialing and having conversations with clients, spreading the message and booking appointments. As a team grows, the need for the phone specialist becomes more obvious. A small team cannot afford a phone specialist, or handle the appointments created by the phone specialist. Where a big team cannot afford the wasted leads that comes from not having a specialist in place to book more appointments. It is a fine line of when you need to add a specialist. In general a quality phone specialist should be able to keep 3-4 full time agents busy trusting that the full time agents are not reliant on 100% of their business coming from the phone specialist. This means most teams need 4-6 active agents before they add a phone specialist to the mix.

Real Estate is the hardest way to make easy money, and being a Phone Specialist is the hardest part of real estate. While there are amazing pluses to the job such as regular hours and often it has a salary plus commission; the frustrations and rejection that come with the job make it one where many who do it feel alone and unsuccessful. It is a job where there is no completion. You never go home at the end of the day having completed all your work. You need to have some personal competition on a daily basis, in the form of minimum goals, and personal bests - day/week/month - numbers in order to maintain sanity and the will to work.

My goal for phone specialists is 2 appointments per calendar day. My personal best was 13 appointments in one day, 32 appointments in one week, and 102 appointments in one month. As a team (of 2 full time and 1 part time) the best week (7days Sunday-Saturday) was an average of 8.46 appointments per day.

These stats are great, fun and give the team something to shoot for and compare themselves against. They can have a bad day, and then look at a weekly goal or monthly goal. They always had something to strive for.

While the focus for a phone specialist must be on booking the appointment, they need to be concerned as much about show up rates, and at the end of the line, the commission part of the job requires that deals are actually completed. Of course, the first thing that needs to occur is the booked appointment so that is where the main focus lies. This is why the "fallback position" on every call needs to be on booking the appointment. If the client does not give us a quality reason not to meet, we need to book an appointment. Next we need to do our very best to ensure that that appointment will actually happen. A good quality reminder call … reminder of the amazing benefits of the appointment not simply the date and time of it, as well as ensuring that the database is kept clean and clear so the agents know what is going on. Then the phone specialist needs to pay a small bit of attention to what is going on with the client through the whole process and be available to help out if possible to ensure that a smooth transaction will occur.

The Phone specialist just like any other specialist needs tools to perform their job. The number one tool for them is the SCRIPT BOOK. I have detailed how to build a script book in one of the chapters, as well as given access to one of my personal Script books should you not have your own plan of attack. They also need a good quality contact management system, a quality phone with a headset, and a fairly quiet space to do their work. The last two tools are the most important, time and patience. This job is both the most rewarding and the most tedious thing you will ever do, your overall success is dependent on your attitude and your control over time and patience.

My last thoughts of this chapter is that I need you the reader to understand that I love this job, I love Real Estate and I love helping people find their passion. There are people who love any and all jobs and they become the best in the world at them. Become that person, find your passion and follow it, and for those tasks that are not your passion, when you can find someone who has that passion and give them the opportunity to live it, the results will astound you.

TIP: *67 / Blocked Call – This should be the usual way you are dialing the phone, only when you cannot reach people try using Cell phones, and office phones without the number being blocked. Remember curiosity killed the cat!

CAREERS AVAILABLE TO THE PHONE SPECIALIST

Quality begins on the inside… and then works its way out.
~~~ Bob Moawad

Since this is a lesser-known aspect of the Real Estate world I thought I'd spend a little time discussing the different career paths that are available to the phone specialist.

The most obvious one is the Solo Agent, since anyone and everyone can be that. For the phone specialist, being a solo agent is often a very trying time, and they tend to be more successful than the average agent, but rarely rise to the level of being a top agent on their own. The best phone specialists can have fits of greatness, but end up not enjoying the face to face and paperwork aspects of the job and the career becomes far less fulfilling.

Next is joining a team. As a full team member a phone specialist can do very well, because they will find business even if none is being provided and will convert the given business at a higher rate. Often the paperwork is reduced and the specialist is free to spend more time doing what they love, booking appointments. However this only increases the face to face time which will still lead to poor job satisfaction levels.

Next is Inside Sales. This is the first career that truly capitalizes on the specialists skills and allows them to do what they do best the vast majority of the time. This career in general pays less than that of a team member overall but has a few major benefits that make the trade a little more equal, such as set working hours, more financial stability as in most instances it comes with a salary portion, plus the benefits of little to no paperwork and no face to face time with clients. The overall job satisfaction is higher; the main sources of frustration come from how the appointments are handled and the feeling of never being done.

The next step in this career is the Inside Sales Manager. They usually get a bit more salary, and share in the commissions from their staff. They will incorporate training and accountability; some more paperwork becomes involved and greater pressures as well. However most people see this as a step up in their life and it provides feeling of running their own department. It helps to satisfy the Real Estate Dream that everyone starts with – being his or her own boss.

The last real opportunity is either Team Leader or Team Manager. Again this is the pinnacle, overseeing the work being done, having a business run under your control. They in general deal with only the problems and challenges that the team faces and this can be very rewarding to those that love the challenge more than anything else. The job gets paid a piece of all the team's commissions and has a salary base as well. For some this is the ultimate job for others they wouldn't be caught dead doing it.

What you have to determine is what is the best career for you, what is it that you want to accomplish and go out and find it.

TIP: Email is not your friend – The phone specialist is exactly that a PHONE specialist, never email a lead or client for any reason, that is someone else's job.

TIP: Organize your calls – Know who is important and who is not, a phone specialist's work is never done, so try to make sure the "best return on time spent" calls are completed each day.

CHAPTER THREE
The Power of Inspiration

Inspiration is the burning desire within oneself to accomplish something. What that accomplishment is? That is up to each individual.
~~~Andy Herrington

This is a topic that is near and dear to me. I believe it is the most important skill any Team Leader, Manager or in fact human can have, the ability to inspire people. This is the only way I know of to harness the amazing results that a quality Phone Specialist can create. Whether it is you who has the phone specialist position, or you are the team leader who is looking to find someone to fill it, understand this truth: *the difference between a telemarketer (and all the stigma that goes with that title) and a Phone Specialist is "inspiration".*

Anyone can motivate someone to do the job, but you will be motivating him or her over and over and over again. You will need to crack the whip and "be the boss" on a regular basis. You will spend as much time babysitting and motivating, as you will hope to save by creating the position in the first place. All you will have at the end of the day is a telemarketer, someone who dials and talks and does the bare minimum and sounds like a robot and ….

However, if you can find and release the inspiration inside the Phone Specialist, you will have someone who creates connections with people and builds up the reputation of your organization. You will have someone who loves to come to work, and knows they are truly making a difference. Then you will only have to create a comfortable work environment where they feel respected and empowered and they will create happy clients and great results. Inspiration you see last a whole lot longer. It is the fishing pole compared to motivation's fish. It provides for a happier workplace for all involved, one where everyone gets his or her own work done.

The inspired specialist will make more calls, have a better conversion percentage and require less supervision. This doesn't mean they will not have bad days, weeks or months, but they should be able to turn things around easier. As a manager or leader, you need to help each person in any position find their inspiration and help them live that inspiration as much as possible. This is the formula for success in real estate. This allows the team leader to spend less time focused on the Phone calls and more on other aspects of the business.

I have written an article that was published in a few magazines over the years and I have put it here, it gives you tips and ideas how to find and capture the inspiration in oneself and in others.

TIP: Vary the Calls – You have different lead sources and different follow up calls, each can break up the monotony of dialing over and over again. When bored, try something new!

ARTICLE: GET INSPIRED AND SELL MORE!
By: Andy Herrington

I have said it before and I will say it again. Motivation is nothing compared to INSPIRATION. I always hear people saying, "You have to get motivated" or "we need more motivation" and the fact is motivation is a short-term thing. Motivate means "to provide with a motive or motives". It is someone providing something to another person. Inspire on the other hand is "to produce or arouse". It is creating something from within. This is where real gain is found. A long term fix because it is a part of the person, not an outside factor.

Think of it this way, you can motivate a child to clean there room by taking away the keys to the car, but how long will that last? If you can find a reason for them to want to clean their room on a regular basis this will create that clean room forever. It is the same as the "Teach a Man to fish" analogy.

Now the best part about this is that becoming inspired and inspiring others is often very similar. *When you find the drive within yourself others are attracted to it, and begin to find the drive in themselves as well.* So you don't simply "do more deals" because you are working harder, you also do more deals because your clients are "inspired" to live their dreams as well.

You have one life – have and create enthusiasm everywhere. Don't just satisfy your clients - overwhelm them with all that you do. Take risks, make mistakes and push your human potential to the utmost limits. When you do, you will no longer chase business you will attract it.

Here are 13 things you can do to find your inspiration and to become an inspiration:

1. Create your Personal goals that include a list of things you'd like to accomplish in your lifetime. Both short term and long-term goals are best. READ THEM DAILY.
2. Create your Business Goals make sure your business goals satisfy your personal goals. READ THEM DAILY.
3. Write down what makes you different and better than your competition. Believe it fully and portray it to everyone you meet.
4. Practice your Scripts, all of them as often as possible. The better you know what to say, the more confidence you will have on saying it and the more opportunities you will look for in order to say it.
5. Tell everyone what your specific sales goals are for the year and keep him or her posted on your progress,

both good and bad. ASK FOR HELP in accomplishing them!

6. Buy a book of inspiration and keep it in your car. Read it daily. This is anything you find inspiring, Mother Teresa, A Pro Athlete, Just a great quote book, anything you know will brighten your mood when needed.

7. Buy a composition notebook write a journal or simply doodle daily. Be creative and allow yourself the ability to do anything. DO NOT CENSURE YOURSELF

8. Invest 15 minutes every day to, watch clips, read books and articles about selling. Don't skip a day. Learning from others is great, and learning something new is often one of the most inspiring things you will ever do, second only to teaching something.

9. Invest 15 minutes daily to plan for the next day. There is nothing more inspiring than starting your day with a written plan or attack- your plan! Make this a daily habit and you'll sell more in less time and have more fun doing it.

10. Surround yourself with the best; hang around with the best in your business/industry. Model their habits and ask them for advice.

11. Break up projects into smaller pieces. Then begin with the second most enjoyable activity and keep the most enjoyable until the end. The more, smaller tasks you do the sooner your big project will be completed.

12. Get a coach. Successful people love helping others to become successful. But what is really most interesting is that the majority of successful people did not get there by themselves.

13. Make time for your loved ones as often as possible. Ask them how you can make their life more successful and try to make that happen, in return they will try to make you as successful as possible.

14. Get and listen to as many ideas as you can from everyone around you. Never limit yourself to your own thoughts and ideas. Ideas are what build and grow. Without a constant discussion about ideas you will stagnate.

15. Implement only the best Ideas, don't get caught in the details and planning and forget to implement!

Inspired people do extraordinary things! What is truly interesting is that they don't search them out; the extraordinary will find to you. The impressive sales numbers, the fame and fortune, these are all by products of all the little things. One of the key little things is Inspiration; this allows you to be able to use the focus and power needed to consistently do all of the other little things that make your skills better and the people around you, family, friends co-workers and clients happier.

TIP: Features TELL, Benefits SELL. Always remember to inform the client about what Benefits they get from what you do. This is what makes people interested in buying.

CHAPTER FOUR

The Mentality of Dialing

Do not fear mistakes. You will know failure. Continue to reach out.
~~~Benjamin Franklin

This is a tough topic; the mental drain that comes from picking up a phone and hearing the dial tone, the pulse tone numbers, the ringing and the answering machines is impressive. It is a huge part of the job of a phone specialist and it can truly be the make or break on any given day.

No matter how good we are at something we are going to have bad days and it is how we respond to those bad days that truly define just how good we are at something. Being a phone specialist is no different; except that any day can be changed from good to bad each time we pick up and dial the phone.

On any given dial we can book an appointment that is obviously so good we can already see the cash in our bank accounts, or talk to a person who obviously has the goal of trying to ruin your life by pointing out every folly that you have and cut you to the quick with their jabs. It is how we respond that separates the specialists from the telemarketers.

The good

We need to feed off the good for energy and passion, but I know people who become immediately complacent after booking an appointment instead of turning that energy into 25 more dials and hopefully 2-3 more appointments. I have seen people who only gain excitement from appointments rather than any and all positive communication with a lead.

The mental issue you will face when you have had early success in a day is 'do I need to work hard still?' This is why having **PERSONAL BEST** numbers is very important. They are used to help people push through the complacent attitude and create unimaginable results, just like athletes do. I have said before that my PB was 13 in a day. This is not possible without harnessing the good energy and focusing it into the work. If my minimum goal is 2 per calendar day, how do I get to 13? Isn't 3 enough, or 5 or surely 10? Honestly my answer would be one day they were. I never imagined that I could book 13 appointments in a day, until I had booked 10 in a day, and I never thought I could do that until I had seen 8 done by someone else I felt I was better than. This is how it is done.

Dialing the phone and the 4 minute mile is the same thing, I personally believe there is someone out there that can book 20 plus appointment in a day, but not if they don't harness the good energy.

The bad

This is the hard one; frankly more bad energy comes through this job than good in most people's eyes. Getting told off, getting hung up on, no answer, answering machines, people who refuse logic, and on and on. There is not a single day (even when you book 13 appointments) where bad energy doesn't creeps in and say hi. But how do we deal with it? I used mantra's to help me a lot. Frankly the mantra(s) I always used was "One more closer to my appointment". That was after a call and "Ok here is my appointment" was the mantra right before a call. Positive self-talk is a truly important skill to have when doing the job of a phone specialist.

In general the real issue is a build up of the bad energy. This can be caused by, a few bad calls in a row, or an hour of answering machines without talking to someone. The after call mantra when done and "believed" is a truly effective tool. It will help you through the vast majority of situations except one.

HUOM – it was my acronym for HUNG UP ON ME in my contact management system. This is easily the most difficult thing to deal with. I have had phone jobs where it happened once an hour and others where it happened once every 3-4 months. The amazing thing was each time it happened it attacked my energy. So here is my advice,

1. Get up and take a walk after that call,
2. Tell yourself that you provided the service the lead needed at the time, they had a bad day, were yelled at by their boss for something that wasn't their fault and that you provide the outlet they needed. 3. Schedule a follow up call for the lead in 1-2 weeks.

By doing this you will take control of the situation. You will be able to see that you helped the lead, which is the main inspiration for doing this job for most people in Real

Estate. Also by knowing that you will call them again you remove their power to 'hurt' you. If I call someone who had HUOM in the notes and they yell and scream and HUOM again, no problems, I'm expecting that, it no longer has any bad energy to it, in fact it can turn the emotional charged call into positive energy that can push me on to more and more calls. It may seem unorthodox, but it worked wonders for me, and in more situations than I can count I booked appointments with people who originally HUOM, those might just be the appointments I am most proud of over the years.

For the phone specialist, repetition and a lack of completion is the real problem. For team leaders, remember that this is a tough job, and reward the phone specialists when you can, even a pat on the back works wonders. For the phone specialist, find something in your life that has a completion factor, in your private life. Puzzles, books, painting, construction, sports whatever will give you that feeling. It will make it "less" needed at work if it exists somewhere, and the long-term result will be more money in your pocket.

TIP: Breaks are needed – On a day that is smooth, two 15 minute breaks and a meal break is all that is needed, but if a caller gets inside your head, take a quick break to refocus and get back to things. Don't let one call ruin 5 more, or worse the rest of the day.

WHEN TO GIVE UP ON A LEAD?

Never give in, never give in, never, never, never, never. In nothing great or small, large or petty, never give in except to convictions of honour and good sense. ~~~ Winston Churchill

This is a question I get all the time. When to give up on a lead? Frankly the first answer that pops into my head is NEVER, but this is unrealistic. So I will Say Close to Never! OK, there are three categories of leads that people give up on and they each have a different time frame of when.

1. Leads who treat me poorly. We have talked a little about them in other parts of the book, so now let me answer, 'when do I give up?'

Your competition will give up on them after the client is rude for the first time. Therefore to be different and better than them, you need to minimally move past this stage.

After they are rude to me the second time, everyone else in Real Estate will give up on them, so to truly be the very best I need to allow them a Three Strike rule. This was always my mentality, and if I am being honest, many times I continued after this solely out of spite, just to cause them a little grief… and I ended up with booked appointments. So for me, my straightforward answer is: Three Strikes and you're out.

2. Leads I cannot get a hold of. I am either getting voicemail or the phone rings with no answer. I will try numerous different tricks here (discussed throughout the book), but what I need to do is try so many times I get sick of seeing their name on my screen. When that happens I move them ahead for a couple weeks and once I have done that 3 times I will give up. My competition will call on average 5 times before giving up, the best in the industry will call 15 times, which means as a phone specialist I will call at least 30 times, more likely 45 times before considering giving up. So for this category, my answer is when I simply cannot look at the name without wanting to poke my eyes out.

3. Leads I talk to that are not doing anything soon. You talk to the lead and they are pleasant and friendly but never seem to be doing anything. Or they say they will be doing something 'soon' every time you talk to them over a long period of time. These people frustrate everyone, they are no real bother but seem to waste my time and probably will never actually move. Your competition will give up on average after 3 conversations, the good agents, after 8 conversations, so to be the very best you can never give up on this type of lead. They talk to you, build rapport and minimally get referrals. If there is a team of specialists, pass them to another team member, but if not, they should never be given up on. So the answer here is NEVER!

So there you have it, simple rule of thumb is if you think should I give up the answer is NO. Only when you are saying, I never want to speak to this person again, I never want to make money from this person, only then should you stop calling them.

To finish off this section, I wrote an article published in REM Magazine in Canada that outlines some tips and tricks to stay focused on dialing the phone, I am going to add it here for you to read and hopefully implement so that more and more dials occur on your phone.

TIP: Avoid Call Display - You have numerous different ways to make your phone look when you call. Blocked, regular, use a cell phone, use your own home phone, some long distance providers have a different way as well. Don't be afraid to mix it up to get ahold of a tricky lead.

TIP: Questions = Information –Information is the greatest tool for the phone specialist and questions equal Information. End your side of the conversation with a question mark every time!

ARTICLE: HOW TO PICK-UP THE PHONE... AND ACTUALLY DIAL IT
By: Andy Herrington

I know this sounds like a silly topic, how to pick up the phone. But you'd be amazed at how difficult a task this really is. If it was a simple case of grab the receiver in your dominant hand and lift, Real estate would be a much easier game than it is. The picking up of the phone is the easy part; the dialing is where the problems begin. So many Realtors, on a daily basis do their very best impression of a 15-year-old nerd calling the head cheerleader. A lot of phones worldwide are stared at all day long, with nothing accomplished.

Dialing the phone is a MENTAL game. You need a good energy level, a positive attitude and confidence in yourself, your message and your ability to handle all situations that might come up. When you have achieved this you will see an amazing thing start to happen. Your ability to pick up the phone and dial will grow. Soon your love of picking up the phone will grow and then it will no longer be a task or a necessary evil, it will be an amazing part of your business and one you look forward to everyday.

Some things to try to help you build your Mental Game:

1. Set a reasonable daily goal for Dials, Contacts and Appointments, and a prize for attaining them.
2. Do not worry about everything on your day timer, only the stuff you can get to – YOU WILL NOT GET TO IT ALL! This is OK.
3. Use a headset when dialing, stand and walk around when dialing, have music in the background (quiet)
4. Role play "out loud" a couple of successful calls prior to picking up the phone.
5. Take a break every 90-120 min for 5-10 min or if a client angers you on a call. Get up walk around take your mind away from calling. When you return refocus and begin dialing again.
6. Know that the hardest Dial is the first one. Call a friendly, or simply use the will power to begin dialing.
7. Watch funny or inspiring videos on youtube.com on your breaks.
8. Affirmations done "out loud" prior to calling or even prior to each call can work wonders. (try – "Helping people", "High Energy, Great Message, Lots of Appointments", "Here is my next appointment" or "I'm an Appointment Booking Machine")
9. Have a mirror in front of you and make sure you are smiling all the time.
10. Have a tally board so your accomplishments are noted and shown to the world. Know what is happening Daily, Monthly and Yearly.

Also read one of the earlier posts on Inspiration versus Motivation. This I hope will help a bit as you begin to get more in the habit of dialing the phone more and more every day.

Lastly, have you completed your own PERSONAL Goals this year? And what goal specifically can be achieved through you making these calls. What is the direct benefit to you to pick up the phone and dial? When you can answer that, you will be well on your way.

TIP: Systems when booking appointments – have a step-by-step system with redundancies in place to ensure everyone who should know, does know about the appointment. Book it in calendars, and send pages and emails letting agents know.

TIP: Questions = Information –Information is the greatest tool for the phone specialist and questions equal Information. End your side of the conversation with a question mark every time!

CHAPTER FIVE

Mirror and Matching

By molding to your client's style, you will be able to provide the quality of service and the results that the client wants.

~~~ Andy Herrington

This is one topic that is a vastly misunderstood part of sales and phone sales. Mirror and matching is a complex sales technique used to put the customer at ease and make them feel as though the sales representative has been a friend for years. I have included an article at the end of this section that I wrote many years ago, which will put a more detailed spin on the overall theme, but I wanted to speak specifically to the Phone specialist's ability to use Mirror and Matching.

The phone specialist obviously is at a disadvantage when it comes to communication, we only have words and how we say the words to convey our message. We do not have body language and facial expression to aid us in getting our point across. This is why the words we use are so important. However what is often overlooked is how those words are spoken. I have said, 'use my script or your script'… as long as the result is the same that is the important thing. This is true because the inflection, tonality and speed of our voice and words convey a massively different message.

It is in these ways that our mirror and matching is key early on in the conversation. However in phone sales we do not always match the client exactly, we actually need to exceed them by one level. Whatever energy and tonal level your lead has on the phone we should be one level above them. More excited and a slightly higher pitch. We then want to slowly increase these levels up to an excited level that would be proper for the call and what we are discussing (as long as the lead is following us as the excitement builds). For example we are helping them buy a house not giving them one for free.

This tool is then augmented by the use of the "BEST" words. Not the proper scripting, that is another chapter, but the correct "extra" and "connector" words.

Extra Words:
We all have our own words that we use repeatedly during conversation; sometimes they have lost all meaning to us. For example, think of a teenage girl (from the 1980's) and the word "like". These words are great tools to have the lead view you as a friend. If you can spot the words that the leads uses, try to work them in naturally to your own conversation. This will get you a more compliant person on the other end of the phone. They are more willing to hear and follow what this "like minded" individual has to say.

Connector Words:
These are the words that mean positive things, they could be Good, Great, Excellent, or even Dude and Beastly. The lead has a word that in their mind means above average, even well above average. For this book I'm going to use GREAT and EXCELLENT. If you poll 100 people I

would say about 60% of people will say Excellent is better than great and others will say Great is better than Excellent and a last group will say they are the same. What we as sales people need to know is which word to say to our lead and client to convey the message we want them to hear. The easiest way to do this is to listen to the words they use and use them right back at them. This ensures we are conveying the message we want the client to hear.

Lastly the mirror and matching lesson that every phone specialist needs to learn is TEMPO. No matter what your normal rate of speech is, we need to ensure that we approximate the leads rate of speech or at most one level quicker. The reason being that if we talk too slowly, the person on the other end will think we are either stupid, or patronizing them. Either way they don't really like us and will not do business with us. If we talk too quickly we will be viewed as "fast talkers", a liar who has something to hide. Again the result is not wanting to do business with us.

So as we a phone specialist, we use these all tools of mirror and matching (inflection, tonality, speed, extra words and connector words) to make our calls smoother, our results better and our pay cheques bigger. We become chameleons and need to remove our need to "be our self" and replace it with the need to "be what the Lead needs us to be". This is often a very difficult transition for many people and it is why most salespeople have specific people they deal with that are so much easier and more fun to deal with. Those people match the salesperson, rather than the salesperson matching the client.

ARTICLE: MIRROR AND MATCHING TECHNIQUES
By Andy Herrington

In Real Estate, gaining and maintaining rapport is a huge key to successfully servicing our clientele and building our business. The quicker we develop it and the stronger the rapport is, the better the relationship is with the client. The better the relationship is, the better they talk about us with their friends and family and the easier the people are to lead toward making a decision. Remember the Golden Rule of Sales – "Treat others the way THEY want to be treated." We have learned about personality types so we can think and behave in a way that they will respond to. Now we need to add to this and continue to develop a stronger rapport with our clients.

Do you remember a time when you had an instant connection with someone? Things just seemed to fit together; you knew what the other was thinking without having to open your mouths. This is the ultimate level of rapport. How easy would our jobs be if we got to only work with people we had this type of connection with?

You would know what your client wanted before they did and could easily direct them down that path.

Well that is what this report is about, how to create a higher level of rapport with our clients. First let's look at what rapport is. Rapport is one of the most important characteristics of unconscious human interaction. It is commonality of perspective, being in "sync", or being on the same "wavelength" as the person with whom you are talking. So how can we figure out how to create instant rapport with people we don't already know? Well we start by looking at people who have rapport and figure out what actions they take when they are together. Anthony Robbins stated, "People who like each other tend to be like each other." This simple statement is proven correct when you look at research done by the Boston University Medical School. Their researchers studied films of people having conversations. They noticed that the people speaking began to UNCONSCIOUSLY co-ordinate their breath patterns, stance, eye blinks, head nods, and more. In fact when the people were monitored, their brain waves were also spiking at the same time. So what were the conclusions of this study?

The key to establishing rapport is to experience the same reality that the other person is living in. To become similar to the client with whom you want rapport. Start off by mirroring and matching the client's physicality, vocabulary, rate and tone of speech. Doing this is a powerful tool. It is a great way of experiencing the client's world.

Remember any observable behaviour can be mirrored and matched; for example:
- Body posture
- Stance
- Hand gestures

- Head movements
- Blink rate
- Facial expression
- Body movements
- Energy level – very important
- Breathing rate
- Vocal qualities
- Vocabulary level
- Key phrases (Catch phrases)
- Type of words used
- Tonality
- Rate of speech
- Volume of speech

And anything else you can observe.

Let's talk about a few of these. Some are rather obvious and others are a little trickier. Some you will already do unconsciously. Others, you will have to forcibly make yourself mirror those traits. These can be used any time you are dealing with people, on the phone, at the movies, in a sales meeting, at a conference, etc.

Vocabulary is a great starting point. Speaking above or below someone is the surest way to damage rapport. Try to use words of a similar level as the words that the client uses, even better, try to use the EXACT same words that the client uses. This is best seen when looking at descriptive words. Try to use your client's words to describe things and they will respond as you would expect them to, for example "excellent". While this word may mean the same as "great" to you, it may not to the client. So if they use the word excellent, you should also use the word excellent.

Next, take into account the way they speak. People will talk the way they think. For example, what do you notice about the following four sentences?

• You have shown me a bright idea on how to proceed and I would like to look into it further.

• You have told me of a way to proceed that sounds good and I would like to hear more about it.

• You have handed me a way to proceed that is on solid ground and I would like to get more of a feel for it.

• You have provided me with a way to proceed that makes sense and I would like to have more details.

The first sentence uses visual words, the second auditory, the third kinesthetic and the fourth uses words that are not sensory based (auditory digital), yet all four sentences convey the same general meaning. If you communicate with someone the way that they think, you will communicate faster, more effectively and be able to direct the client in a more efficient manner. You will also create a connection to that person and they will begin to think that you see the world as they do. They will trust you more and want to be around you. They will look to you for advice and share more about themselves than they would under different circumstances.

Listen to the tone and rate of speech that the client uses. Do they talk fast or slow, are they loud or quiet? Do they have an accent, or staccato tone? This is not about having a deep voice or a high pitch; it is about how they talk. People respond well to similar speech patterns. Think about how children can move from one part of the world to another and quickly pick up the new accent; they do it to fit in, to be accepted.

The final item with regard to vocally matching people is backtracking. Backtracking is active listening using the mirror and matching tools. As you take in information from your client, repeat it back to them using similar language, without judgment. You will create an environment where the client will feel safe and respected and they will feel you understand them and really listen to them. You want to use similar language and include the same words when necessary. You are looking to capture the essence of what the person is saying, not a verbatim rehash of what they said. You can then ask for clarification on any points, and also provide them with an opportunity to correct you if you misunderstood something. If this happens, make sure to backtrack again once they are finished to ensure you're on the same page.

We can use what I have discussed everywhere, including on the phone. But in order to create even better rapport when you actually meet the client, add physical mirror and matching to the vocal mirror and matching. This will truly create a strong bond. Physically attempt to take the same stance and posture as the client. Sit the way they sit, cross your legs like them, place your hands in a similar spot. Try to breathe at the same rate as them and blink at the same time as them. Yes this seems very mechanical; however you should not be looking to do all of these with the same person. A few are enough to accomplish your goal. Also this is not like the 'Mirror' game you might have played in school, where you attempt to do the same actions at the same time. If they change posture, wait 5-10 seconds then you switch to match. Move at the same rate as them as well, if they adjust quickly, you should also. If they do it slowly, you will too. If they talk with their hands, you should also talk with your hands. Use similar hand gestures and match their speed and intensity. Hold your head the way they do. When you are fully mirroring and matching you will be sitting the same way, using the same gestures, speaking at similar speed and volume, in a similar tone and you will begin to breathe at the same rate. At this point you will have a good rapport with the client and you may even be able to lead them and their behaviour.

You can try to cross-match with a client as well. For example, if they are someone who consistently straightens their glasses, but you do not wear glasses, you can straighten your tie or play with your ring or straighten your watch. The key is to behave in a similar manner as the client and make them feel comfortable with you. The more comfortable they are, the better your relationship will be and the easier the transaction will become.

The more you practice these techniques, the more natural it becomes. Start off by mirroring and matching while watching TV, specifically interview shows and chat shows. Get yourself into doing things smoothly and easily. Then begin to try it out in real conversations. As you become better, begin to do this on the phone and on your appointments.

Many people find the idea of mirroring someone very uncomfortable and they feel that they are trying to trick or take advantage of the person. What you need to remember is that this is a natural part of rapport building, and that you do it unconsciously everyday with people you are drawn to. We are not lucky enough to only work with those people. In fact we will find that those 'troublesome' clients will become fewer and farther between when we can help create the rapport that is so obviously lacking. If someone else does something that you wish you were better at, try mirroring them and seeing what they see. You will find that you become better at that same activity.

TIP: The Power of an Apology – if you made a mistake, or even if the lead/client just thinks you have, an apology is a very effective tool to calm a tense moment. Allowing you to build rapport quicker than any other tool available to you.

CHAPTER SIX
Philosophy of Leads

Your philosophy determines whether you will go for the disciplines or continue the errors.
~~~Jim Rohn

When building a script and spending time on the phones, you will begin to see that one of the most important tools you can have and use is an understanding of the philosophy of converting a lead to an appointment. This is an understanding of how to get people to agreed to meet with a sales representative even thought they likely would prefer not to.

The first step in the philosophy is to stop seeing yourself as a Salesperson. Instead view yourself as an ADVISOR. Someone whose job it is to advise the client of the marketplace and how to go about accomplishing their goal of homeownership. This is an important mental shift and can be used on the phone and in presentations. This is a key shift that will position yourself to earn more money and have less stress in your life. Advisors do not take ownership of prices or negotiations, they do not make promises, Advisors make observations, share information and provide advice so the client can make a quality decision, but whatever the client decides it is their own decision.

Once we have made that key shift in our minds, we can look at some of the philosophical tools we can use to our and the clients advantage.

      1. Philosophy of Counteraction
      2. Philosophy of Why
      3. Philosophy of Consistency
      4. Philosophy of Social Proof
      5. Philosophy of Reduced Effectiveness
      6. Philosophy of Previous Dealings
      7. Philosophy of If

Lets review each of these and how we can use them to our advantage.

Philosophy of Counteraction

Newton's 3rd law states - for every action there is an equal and opposite reaction. For sales, this is an understanding that our actions will result in counteractions from the client. In fact even a perceived action will create a counteraction from your client. According to Dr. Robert Cialdini, one of the most widespread and basic norms of human culture is counteraction. His rule is that if someone does some action for you, you will want to do a counteraction in return. This is commonly known as "you scratch my back I'll scratch your back". This sense of obligation ensures that relationships grow, and that transactions and exchanges that are valuable occur.

A favourite and profitable use of counteraction is to provide the action before asking for anything in return. You can see this being used by charities when they include the gift of address labels in hope that you will donate to the charity in the future. Although the "gift" is relatively inexpensive it plays upon our inherent need to reciprocate even when the gift was not asked for or even not wanted at all.

There are many ways that you can use this concept as a phone specialist. At the beginning of a call let the lead know you have done something for them, in return they will likely answer some questions. When Reminding a client of an appointment let them know you have done the prep work for them, they will be less likely to cancel an appointment.

Philosophy of Why

This is an understanding that people do not respond well to being told they "need to do something" without knowing WHY. As a phone specialist our job is to convince the lead to meet with a sales representative and they do not immediately want to do this. We need to explain WHY it is important to them to meet with us.

The Why is how to inspire people to action, but too often salespeople explain the features of a product or service which is explaining what a client gets, not why they should get it. Advisors inform a client of the benefits the client will get from following a specific action; this is why the client should act.

Philosophy of Consistency

People like to be consistent, so if they say yes, they want to continue saying yes. If they say no they want to continue to say no. A consistent approach is always useful. Small yes's can become a big yes. Now this doesn't specifically mean only the word yes. If they agreed with you that what you are saying is good, or right than when you ask for something they would usually not see as a positive, it will seem more reasonable. For the phone specialist, asking the right questions and making the right offers, then following with asking for an appointment creates a better opportunity to book an appointment that the client is a little afraid of.

Philosophy of Social Proof

People do not like to be the first person to use your service. They want to know that it is somewhat exclusive and they are better than others if they do use it, but having testimonials and a history of success will help you. Sometimes for the phone specialist this is a bit harder to incorporate, but reminding a lead "because of the sheer volume of business we do…" can remind them that there is a history behind your service.

In todays world much of this Social Proof needs to be found on the Internet, in the form of social media. Many times your client will not ask you, or give you the opportunity to provide social proof they will have gone in search of it first. As a phone specialist directing them to places to find the social proof is a good way to end a call in all circumstances.

Philosophy of Reduced Effectiveness

This is the understanding that even when we do a great job of inspiring our leads to action, we will soon hang up the phone and our energy and positive words will slowly dissipate. They will talk to other people and those people will likely be less than positive about the action the client has decided to do. Also the human brain will get involved and begin going through all the scenarios including things that are highly unlikely and highly unsatisfactory or even scary. This means the client becomes less and less interested in performing the action they agreed to do. The next time you speak with them be prepared to revitalize their interest and do not be surprised or get frustrated that this is lack of inspiration is occurring. For phone specialists, I recommend speaking to a lead again to remind the lead about the importance, excitement and of course the benefits of the appointment any time that the meeting is more than 1 sleep away from when you originally booked the appointment.

Philosophy of Previous Dealings

People will judge future dealings with those that have happened in the past. This is truly important for the phone specialist. Know that our call is influence by all previous calls the lead has had from any salesperson in the past. This includes other "telemarketers" and other Real Estate people. You need to set yourself apart and understand that the client will not immediately be open and loving toward you. So do not expect them to be your friend, do not attempt to 'create rapport' on the first call, be business like and make sure the client understands you do not wish to waste their time, but are there to help advise them in regard to their upcoming real estate transaction. Also important is to leave them with a good overall impression of you and your company should you not get an appointment, as this will affect your future dealings with the client. Remember that sadly this good impression is counteracted by the many bad impressions that other telemarketers and real estate people are going to make before you talk again.

Philosophy of If

'If' is a very important and powerful word for the phone specialist. One of the worst habits we can have on the phone is attempting to pin down a lead on exact time frame or exactly where the client wants to go to early in the process. People are afraid of absolutes because they may not be right (goes back to the philosophy of consistency). However, taking away the absoluteness of the situation with a simply little "IF" can create all the difference. Use questions like the following to determine timing and location.

• If you did move where would you go?
• If you did move when would you do it?
• If everything worked out perfectly when would it happen?

When used correctly and consistently you will see a steady increase in the number of appointments, the number of attended appointments, the number of contracts and the number of deals. These philosophies are impressive tools that can vault any salesperson into the realm of the TRUSTED ADVISOR. And believe me, trusted advisors get more referrals and make a whole lot more money at the end of the day.

TIP: Notes are your friends – Take notes while calling, personally I did them on paper but have seen people do them with a computer to. Then take the time after the call to formulate your notes in your CRM. A great note can help you build rapport next time!

The Myth of "The Quality of the Leads"

If you see the gold in the mountain, you will work hard and take the time needed to mine it out, if you see the rock, you will say it is a waste of your time. ~~~ Andy Herrington

This is something that I hear with everyone I coach, meet or hear from via email or Facebook or twitter. It is this worry about the Quality of the Leads they getting or generating. "Are they good enough?" "They are crap!" "There is nothing happening here"… I hear it all. And while there are differences in leads in regard to quality of the conversion percentages, the quality of leads are solely what YOU believe them to be. Let me write that again in big letters too, THE QUALITY OF THE LEADS ARE SOLELY WHAT YOU BELIEVE THEM TO BE!

But first things first, to understand the leads and how to best convert them, first we need to understand the Buyer Cycle

The Buyer Cycle

We need an understanding of the normal cycle a buyer has from first thinking about making a move until they actually buy a home. In North America that cycle is approximately 14 weeks (3.5 months). During this cycle the buyer goes through 4 phases,

- Phase one is "Locating and Reading Information,"
- Phase two is "Looking at Pictures of Houses,"
- Phase three is "Looking Inside Houses,"
- Phase four is "Buying a homc."

Phase 1 takes about 2 weeks. During this phase the buyer searches the Internet for information on how to buy and does a wide search for homes, trying to find a supremely good deal while reading up on what the steps in the process are. They are not willing to raise their hand or call a real estate agent or company. They are not even sure they will buy at this point. They often fill out forms to get information sent to their email. Traditional Marketing garners no leads from this phase.

Phase 2 is 4-6 weeks in length. Here they are looking only at listing pictures online and in newspapers and magazines. They are still a little afraid to contact a Real Estate person, in any manner outside of email. Unless they see a super deal they are happy just becoming aware of the marketplace. Traditional marketing does not garner many leads here.

Phase 3 is 6-8 weeks in length, they are willing and need a real estate agent, they continue to look in newspapers and on line and call Real Estate agents, they head to Open Houses and talk to agents, they will sign Buyer agency once they choose an agent. Traditional marketing capitalizes on this group.

The last phase is 1-2 weeks in length, buying a home, from offer to firm. They are past marketing and have chosen an agent.

All leads fall somewhere in the buyer cycle. Even people looking to list their home for sale normally start their process in the buyer cycle, and the listing occurs in the final 8-10 weeks of the cycle. But since all leads fall into this cycle, they all must have a similar "quality" level; it is now just a time issue.

We all know someone who is an impeccable cold caller, and is truly successful in picking up the phone, calling the phone book, booking appointments and making money. There is no doubt that in quality of conversion percentages that cold calling is the lowest end of the spectrum, however, the leads themselves are free and you have basically an infinite amount of leads, all you need is the ability to do the work and the time to do it and the results will come.

With that in mind, lets look at the spectrum in regard to average conversion percentages (from phone specialists not active full time salespeople) to APPOINTMENT from a bunch of different types of leads this is a conversion from lead to appointment over a period of 12 months.

Conversion Percentage
- Cold calling - 1%
- Farming – 2-3%
- Unbranded Internet Leads – 15% plus
- Unbranded Print Leads – 20% plus
- Branded Internet Leads (third party "i.e. Head office leads") – 30% plus
- Branded Internet Leads (first party "from your website") – 38% plus
- Branded Print Leads – 57% plus
- Referral Leads (business referral) – 75% plus
- Referral Leads (client referral) – 93% plus
- Repeat Leads - 97% plus

So with this in mind, if you have been doing a business based on repeat and referral leads for a long period of time and then add in Internet leads of any caliber and expect a similar conversion, you will become frustrated with "the quality" of the leads. However, you may be getting a good quality conversion and not even realize it. Each lead type needs to viewed in its own light not compared to other types of leads.

Remember how it was at the beginning of trying to build your repeat and referral business, it did not happen overnight. It takes years to build up that business and most new Real estate agents might get a couple repeat and referral leads in their first couple of years. The same build up occurs with any other type of lead you generate.

If you get 100 unbranded Internet leads today, having never dealt with them before, I would expect a conversion percentage (to appointment) of 6-8% over the year if you work the leads properly. Not the 15% you will get to over time as you become proficient at dealing with the leads and doing the follow up calls properly. You also might not see a single appointment for 3 or more months. This is because of where on the "Buyer Cycle" the Internet leads come from. With Internet lead generation we are now getting leads from phase 1 and 2, in the past those leads were much more rare. The lead is much more skeptical and skittish at this point and booking an appointment the first time we speak is a lot more difficult. These leads are more about follow up and providing that information and advice that we need to as an advisor. To get our conversion percentage up we need to become more understanding, less pushy and we need to have amazing follow up skills.

So you might be asking since there are obvious differences in the conversion percentage, how can I say that Lead Quality is a myth? Conversion percentage is only one factor in determining quality. Leads also need to be judged on their Coast Effectiveness, amount of supply and the time involved in converting them. Then putting all of this together, we can truly determine the quality of the lead. So lets look at the average cost per lead for those same types of leads.

Cost Effectiveness:
• Cold calling - FREE
• Farming – $50-120 (note: cost per appointment as lead itself is free, but ad campaign is costly)
• Unbranded Internet leads – $7-10
• Unbranded Print Leads – $15-20
• Branded Internet leads (third party) – $2-7

- Branded Internet leads (first party) – $15-30
- Branded Print Leads – $120-150
- Referral leads (business referral) – $50-200 (sometimes FREE)
- Referral Leads (client referral) – $200-400
- Repeat Leads - $200-400

Amount of Supply
- Cold calling – High supply
- Farming – Fixed supply (by choice)
- Unbranded Internet leads – High supply
- Unbranded Print Leads – High supply
- Branded Internet leads (third party) – Low Supply
- Branded Internet leads (first party) – Medium Supply
- Branded Print Leads – Medium Supply
- Referral leads (business referral) – Very Low Supply
- Referral Leads (client referral) – Low Supply
- Repeat Leads - Low Supply

Time needed
- Cold calling – Very High time
- Farming – High time
- Unbranded Internet leads – Medium time
- Unbranded Print Leads – Medium time
- Branded Internet leads (third party) – Medium Time
- Branded Internet leads (first party) – Medium Time
- Branded Print Leads – Medium Time
- Referral leads (business referral) – Low Time
- Referral Leads (client referral) – Low Time
- Repeat Leads - Low Time

Now some of these numbers may seem surprising, but this is the truth. The cost to create Repeat and Referral leads is High and the supply is low, but based on the low time needed plus the high return it is absolutely worth the cost. Farming when done really well is very expense per appointment but can have a very good return on investment over time. The lead itself is free and you can farm to as many as you want but once we make that choice the supply becomes fixed. The ad campaign to build the reputation is where the costs arise and the time needed to convert the leads especially early on in the process is often as high as cold calling.

So when we really look at conversion versus cost we will see that all leads are of similar quality. High supply leads cost less and take more time, where low supply leads cost more but take less time. It is simply a matter of the time I spend with those leads to convert them. The key for any business is to find what is seen as gold and then go to work to mine it.

We must to stop the discussion of the quality of the leads and instead determine do I have the time to convert them or not. If I am making a sufficient living from what I have, I don't need to add more leads or new types of leads. However, if I do need different types of leads, I need to look at cost vs. time and figure out what works best for my business. And evaluate those leads based on others like it, not a completely different category.

Lastly, say this to yourself: "If I am adding leads and not converting them, the problem is with me not the leads." This is the only truth about leads that really matters.

TIP: Don't Ask "How are you" - on the next 3 million + calls you make, the person you are talking to is "FINE" there, now you know. You do not need to ask them.

CHAPTER SEVEN

Realistic Expectations

What is destructive is impatience, haste, expecting too much, too fast.
~~~ May Sarton

As you become a phone specialist or have added one to your team, it becomes increasingly obvious that there needs to be goals and expectations put on the role. We have already talked about "when to give up on a lead' which is a common worry, but throughout this chapter, I want to discuss what the phone specialist's day should look like and how to know what has occurred during that day.

When should I call?

Weekday:

8:30am-11:00am: — are the best morning hours to call, however you run the risk of bothering people as they are getting ready for the day. It is also a good time for people with work phone numbers as often people are looking for a way to procrastinate before starting at work.

11:00am – Noon: This is a difficult hour to reach people, if at work they are trying to get some work done before lunch so the morning has not been a complete waste, or so they can get out for lunch.

Noon-3:00pm: A time to call people are on their lunch break or just returned to work and looking for a distraction before starting to work again.

3:00-5:00pm: – is the WORST time to try and speak to people – if at work they are now getting on task to get things complete before they have to go home, if at home, the kids are returning from school and they are trying to deal with them.

5:00-7:00pm: – This is a tough time and you will get "dinnertime" calls, where you will speak to people but they will have a higher level of frustration because they are driving home or sitting at the dinner table.

7:00-8:00pm: – A great hour to call, some left over dinner time people but in general more relaxed and ready to discuss other thoughts in their lives such as real estate.

8:00-9:30pm: – Single best time to call during the week. 8 to 9 is normal and when you are on a roll throwing in the extra 30 min is well worth it. Any later and you are bothering people who are in bed. This 1-hour or 1:30min of calling is worth 2-3 hours at any other time of the day.

Weekend and Stat holidays:

Saturday:
9:00-12:00 – this is the best time to get a hold of people these hours are equal to the 8:00-9:00pm time slot during the weekday.

12-9pm – As long as people are still answering the phone, dial! The nicer the weather the tougher the afternoons and evenings become.

Sunday:

The rules for Sundays depend on your area. If you are in a heavily religious area, calling on Sundays can offend some people. In fact depending on the religion in the area this "offensive period" could happen at other times of the week as well. Know your area don't call when people will be offended. Other than this, Sundays are the same as Saturdays except I would start a little later in the day as many people like to sleep in on Sundays.

Stat Holidays:
These can be the best days of the year to reach people, and typically they are is a great mood. Obviously the more 'religious' the day the more angry people are with 'telemarketers' of any type. That said some of my very best days were during Stat holidays. I strongly recommend coming in and calling on those days.

How long on any given day?

In general a Phone specialist should look at doing six 6-hour shifts every week. Mostly nights and weekends with some daytime calling to ensure we are trying to reach people we can't get ahold of throughout the entire day. (3-9pm, 9am-3pm shifts) You should take at least two 15 min breaks and one 30min break for a meal.

How many leads?

A quality phone specialist needs 150-200 leads a month to turn around the results we are looking for. However each month this number should fluctuate depending on the size of the follow up business in their database. The phone specialist should have 300 plus names to dial any given day. An Active agent would require between 30-50 new leads a month if there is no Phone Specialist help available. Beyond this number and the Active agent will make a sufficient living from dealing with only the very best leads, and will discard any lead that needs follow up or future effort.

How often to call a new lead before giving up?

The following is the requirements I made on my phone specialist staff in the past to get a hold of a lead.

When given a new lead the phone specialist will make three attempts a day for seven days. For clarification that is days of calling so if they work a six-day shift it should take approximately 8 days to accomplish this (21 calls). Then once a day for the next 7 days (total 28 dials), at this point they can leave a voice mail. Then they should put the lead off to dial seven days in the future. Then they should dial it once a day for fourteen more days (total 42 dials), and then if they want they could give up on that lead as unreachable. This provides a level of expectation that no Active Agent could ever accomplish. Only a phone specialist can do this, and it allows the specialist the ability to "suck the marrow from the bones" and allows the team to get more out of the current marketing budget.

If we speak to the lead, in general I would rarely give up ever. To reiterate the key point made in the "When to give up on a lead" chapter, even those people being rude to me will speak to me one or two more times. I simply need to speak to them when they need my services and me, and they will cease to be rude, and book an appointment.

Dry spells happen!

This is an inevitability of the phone specialist, a period of time where nothing seems to go right. No one is meeting with you, the no show rate is through the roof and our own mentality begins to fade. This is the true test of a phone specialist.

How to over come these dry spells.
The first and most important thing to do is CONTINUE DIALING. It is also the hardest thing to do. The lower the results go, the lower our drive to dial the phone. Remember that when things are going bad, your 'dial 'numbers should be higher. You need to push through the pain.

Next you need to be self-evaluating. After each call replay the call and determine if you like what you were saying. Use your script book here and be overly critical of your own work. Get back to basics and use the scripts word for word. Becoming complacent in scripting is the leading cause for most dry spells. Read your scripts a few times before calling and truly prepare yourself just as you did in the beginning.

Get the right attitude, even if it is fake. I am a big believer in mantra's and affirmations. Say to yourself that you love the job, love to dial and are about to book an appointment before every call. Force a smile on your face, and force positive energy out your mouth when you speak. Be excited about helping people again. It all seems a bit silly but works wonders time and time again.

Lastly know that you are not alone, dry spells happen to all of us and the best news is that the flip side is about to come, your "Midas days', you know the man with the golden touch, where everything will go right and those are the days we all live for.

TIP: 8-9pm – is the single greatest hour of dialing in any weekday, it is worth 2 hours of dialing at any other time. Don't give up too early!

TRACKING YOUR TACO!

Risk comes from not knowing what you are doing.
~~~ **Warren Buffet**

This is the toughest simple thing to do. It is true, it has a feeling of big brother is watching, but without the right tracking nothing else that a phone specialist does is worth it's salt. This is the tool that allows you to know your results and in doing so allows you to look for ways to improve things, and project what the future will hold. Without it you are just dialing a phone and hoping it will all work out. With it you are able to predict results and determine how much you want to make each year and accomplish it.

Tracking is very simple; I believe it is still best accomplished with pen and paper on a simple form on a daily basis. This paper form may then be compiled into an electronic mass tracking system. Someone more suited to the task, not a salesperson or a phone specialist, should do this. The form must be completed daily but could be built to accommodate a weeks worth of information and therefore handed in once a week.

For tracking purposes we need to know what to look at and what should be expected on a day in and day out basis. A minimal amount of tracking would entail "Tracking your TACO". This would be your Talked to, Appointments booked, Contracts Signed and Offers. However as you become busier and larger you will Track more then just those items. Attempts, Talked to, Buyer Interviews, Appointments, Messages left, Call Backs (from messages), Follow up calls booked, cancellations, no shows and DEAD Leads. I will discuss what you should expect from the most important categories as your phone specialist becomes more and more effective. However, first I will define the terms I use to ensure you and I have the same understanding regarding my terms.

Attempts:
This is a generic term and refers to the number of times the phone is picked up in an attempt to speak with someone regarding real estate. So this would be an outgoing dial, whether the person answered the phone or not and incoming calls that you answered looking to talk to someone. One can also (an should also) have more than one dial per day for any specific person. This is not looking to determine how many people did I try to reach but how many attempts did I make to try and reach someone.

Talked To:

This is a generic term referring to the number of people I spoke to "about Real Estate" with the ability to book an appointment during the tracking period. If I call a number and speak to the wrong person this is not a contact. If I answer a phone looking for a lead and speak with an agent inquiring on behalf of his client, this is not a contact, but both examples would be a dial.

Buyer Interview:

This is a generic term for a face-to-face meeting where the ultimate goal should be to book an Appointment. (eg. – a showing, an Open house meeting) This is a new way to look at these huge time wasters in Real Estate. The most successful agents and teams have eliminated this from their tasks.

Appointment:

This is a generic term referring to a face-to-face meeting with a client with the ultimate goal and ability to sign a contract for services, specifically a Buyer Representation Agreement or a Listing agreement. NOTE: a showing without a meeting before or after is not an appointment.

Cancellations:

When a lead cancels a previously booked appointment before the appointments scheduled time. This may occur by telephone, email or even during a Reminder call. If an appointments date and time are simply changed that is not a cancellation, however if the client cancels then we later rebook the appointment it will count as a cancellation and a new appointments for statistical purposes.

No Show:

When a client does not show up for a previously scheduled appointment without informing the agent beforehand. This is a part of the Real Estate business and any Phone Specialist worth their salt has a no show rate, the goal is to keep it as low as possible. Often this is a sign of booking a lead for an appointment too soon or pushing certain personality types to hard for a face-to-face appointment.

Messages Left: A voice mail is left for a lead. For me this is a major waste of time and should be used VERY sparsely. If a message is left I recommend the following script. "Hi {Client first name} it's {first name} call me back at {Number}."

Callbacks: Directly from the voice mail message left

Follow up Calls booked – A lead is spoken to, and we determine a time in the future when we should call again to check up on the status of their plans.

DEAD leads: A lead I no longer wish to contact ever again. Examples – Wrong number, already bought and sold, excessively rude. These leads should be forwarded to the team leader (they should also be few and far between).

Now we are on the same page about what the terms mean, lets look at what an effective completed tracking sheet should look like.

A phone specialist with a quality work ethic and the leads to dial should be making 160-220 dials a day based on a 6-hour shift. They should have talked to 30-50 people a day.

They should be expected to book 2 appointments per calendar day ... a month with 30 days = 60 appointments, regardless of the number of days they work (unless of course they go away on vacation). Cancelations are a part of business and should be kept under 15%, while no shows will fluctuate depending on the expertise of the specialist, and the stage of the leads in the buying cycle. A phone specialist who is using mainly Internet and stealth advertising leads can expect a no show rate in the 20-40% range fluctuating month to month.

These numbers will give you a guideline to know if the phone specialist is working hard enough and smart enough. Some people will exceed these numbers and some will fall short, you need to pick the "important ones" to you and make sure they are being met. Tracking can be used to emphasize a point as well, such as the waste of time leaving messages is. As the Phone specialist proves himself or herself, the need for exact number of dials is relaxed, accept a rough estimate of dials. This is usually 2-3 months into the phone specialist's tenure. At this point I will also start tracking Appointments Met, and No Show Appointments, while removing the Messages left and Call Backs from Messages.

At the end of the day this tracking will allow you to forecast earnings for the phone specialist as well as the team. It will allow you to know the cost effectiveness of what you are doing and make budgeting a far easier task. Without it, you are flying blind and just hoping that things will work out.

TIP: Stand up and be heard – Standing and walking about is a great way to sound and be energetic, especially when your energy is waning.

CHAPTER EIGHT

The Importance of Follow-up Calls

My greatest point is my persistence. I never give up in a match. However down I am, I fight until the last ball. My list of matches shows that I have turned a great many so-called irretrievable defeats into victories. ~~~ Bjorn Borg

This is a simple topic but one that 99.9% of all Real Estate people fail to do from time to time. It is the true turning point in each and every Real Estate business out there. The quality and consistency of follow up skills and follow up time spent is directly linked to the cost effectiveness in our marketing.

Whenever I speak on this topic I lead into it as a topic that will allow us to make more money without spending any more dollars. It is truly this important in each and every one of our businesses. Now I am not the first to write about the power of follow up, nor will I be the last, but for Real Estate I wanted to specifically target who and how often we should be doing follow up. Specifically the PHONE follow up - I personally never believe that Email or Mailers count as a contact.

Whenever we create an abundance of leads, we will end up being able to put those leads into two categories. Those we spoke to, and those we didn't. For those we spoke to we have four additional categories;

- Those we booked an appointment with
- Those doing something in near future
- Those doing something in the far future
- Those who were rude to us

This is a total of 5 groups of people and the very best organizations in the world have a Follow up protocol for each group.

One simple thing anyone can implement is the final question to ask any lead that is not booking an appointment. The direct quote, "I love to keep in touch with my clients, when would be a good time for me to follow up with you?" is a great tool to help determine which group the lead falls into. Please note, I'm not asking IF I can follow up, but WHEN I should. They will give me a time frame, and sometimes it will be very different from what I was thinking. This time frame allows me to place them in the correct category. Once we know what category they belong in, we can determine our protocol. Each organization needs to build their own, and there is no perfect system, but I will give my thoughts on each group and how often they should be followed up with.

Booked Appointment:
Obviously for those that booked an appointment with us, we hope that the appointment was good and the client signed with us and at that point other protocol takes over. But what about the appointments where they didn't sign with us? When should we call them back, how often and what should we say. This is the most over looked group with the most potential up side amongst the follow up calls.

Real Estate people tend to give up after meeting with people if they do not get what they want. Each lead should have a follow up plan built after the appointment with weekly to monthly calls as needed. I would also add a hand written note to be dropped off at their home within 48 hours. Some emails can be used, but not as a replacement for calling.

Near Future:

For the leads with near future business we need to have a plan with ever other week to monthly calls and rapport building techniques. This is the group where most follow up is currently done. However most organizations do not contact them frequently enough. Nor do they provide some free information or other "(free) gifts" to help build rapport. As well as an Email Drip campaign targeted to them.

Long Term Future:

For the leads in the far future, these should be contacted two to four times a year, the calls should be friendly and not pushy, they should leave the lead with a good positive feeling about dealing with you in the future. This doesn't mean we are not trying to set appointments, but many of these appointments will be in the future not today. This is a very often overlooked category where the future of our business lies while we cannot be caught up spending hours and hours of time here, a little effort can go a long way with this group of people. Their own Email drip "touch" campaign here works in conjunction with the calling.

Rude and Not Talked to:

Now the last two groups in my mind should be treated the same, and we can add in any other leads we have given up on for any reason. These leads need to be placed in a big batch and contacted in two different situations.

First whenever a new person joins the organization, their first few weeks on the phones should be dealing with the leads that no one has gotten ahold of or that were rude to us in the past or that we have given up on over time. These calls are for training purposes, and appointments are gravy, and in fact every time I have seen this done, appointments are booked from this group of "misfit leads".

The other situation is whenever we are having a lull in business or a lull in lead production. This group of leads always seems to produce, time changes people and it is amazing what an impact on our business these leads can have.

Something to think about is the fact that 66% of the appointments that are available in the leads we create are available **only** through follow up. Yet most organizations are extremely lacking in follow up systems. This category truly is the greatest place that we can make changes to see huge results in the bottom line without any huge investment of dollars. It is the first place that every organization should look to improve their skills and the most cost effective way to improve our bottom line.

TIP: Use a headset – This will make you sound better, and allow you to do more while on the call. Having your hands free simply to gesture will make you sound more conversational and less salesman like.

CHAPTER NINE

Scripting

Scripting is only as good as the speaker's belief in the message. Who wrote the words you use doesn't matter as much as do you believe in what they say.
~~~Andy Herrington

Scripting seems to be an evil word in many circles, but I know that whether or not you realize it, you are using a script each and every time you are on the phone. Over the days, weeks, months and years you have learnt what works and what doesn't and have formed some version of a script. What is really in debate is the extent of the script, how exact you are each and every time and who wrote the script. Personally, I have used other people's scripts and have written my own. The results have varied and not in the way many people would like to believe. Neither the 'do you own thing' nor the 'My script is the only right script' people will be happy when I say that I have had equal success from both version and equal failures from both versions.

What I have found is that there are five truisms to scripting no matter what you do, or where you are and I'd like to share them with you.

A script written down is far better than one in your head.

Once you write something down, you can set about a. learning it word for word and b. improving it over time. The first step in any scripting process must be to write it out in full. I am amazed at how many people fight scripting however they possess great scripting, they just have failed to write it out, and because of this their skills diminish over time and they have no way to check back and figure out what they are doing differently.

Belief in the message is the single biggest key in the success of any script

Ever wonder why some scripts work and others don't. Or how one person has amazing success saying something but it just doesn't work for you? Well it all comes down to believing in what you say. Belief in the Message; it is so important that it is my Tagline on my blog. People want to listen to someone who speaks with passion and sincerity, not a automaton that can easily spit out the "right words". So no matter how good the script is, if you do not believe 100% in the words on the page, the meaning behind them and that they are in the very best interests of the client, the success rate you will have will be miniscule.

"Short scripts require word precision, long scripts require message precision."

A short script such as a telephone script require word for word accuracy, where as longer presentational style scripts need to allow the flexibility for message to message accountability.

WORD FOR WORD is needed for these short scripts as even the smallest change can have a huge impact on the results of the script. In fact, small words have greater importance than you given them credit for. In most instances the changes from original script to "personal version" involves what the salesperson sees as unimportant changes. They remove "insignificant words" or change them to a "similar" word. As a scriptwriter let me say that the words the salesperson thinks are important usually are not, and the ones they change are the psychological keys to the success of the script. For example picture a script with the following phrase – "It will update you…" and someone changes that to say, "I will send …" these are seemingly harmless changes, but psychologically speaking the message is drastically different. "I vs. It" – One instance is referring to an automated process versus one where the person will perform a duty. For many clients they are afraid to inconvenience someone else and will say no to an offer with I and yes to an offer with It. "Send versus update" – Send can be interpreted as the whole list each time, rather than update which will convey only changes to the list this can get a client to see a dramatic difference in the offer from what they can get themselves. Lastly, removing the word "you". This is the most common and surprising thing I see in "personalized scripts." You and any version of that word is the most important word in any script. The more you can say it without becoming a crazy person the better. Less 'I's' and more 'you's' is a great thing. It lets your client know that you worry about them and their needs far more often than you do for yourself and your needs.

Tracking is 100% necessary in order to improve a script.

Phone Scripts need to be memorized, internalized, and used for a period time where the results are tracked before looking for ways to improve and change them. Learning the scripts to a point where you can self evaluate if you are using them WORD FOR WORD each and every time you are on the phone, only then can we determine what the exact results are for a script. Then we can make MINOR changes one by one over time and see if there are repercussions or improvements. Most script changes result in a worse performance, certainly in the short term since the belief in the new script has not solidified in us yet. Tracking new scripts takes time and patience and too many people make sweeping changes or make changes too often to get a good handle on the exact results. Most script changes should be tracked weekly for a minimum of one month before any level of evaluation on its success or failure can be determined. Also you should only track one script change at a time. You can see just how long and involved it can be to implement fresh changes to a scripting platform. This is one reason why many people find a script and just stick with it, until it doesn't work anymore.

All scripts need to have a Customer Driven Approach or they will not work!

This is one that we hear over and over, but I am amazed how rarely it is actually utilized. "W.I.F.M. (What's in it for me) is the radio station everyone listens to" is practically a mantra of every sales trainer I have ever spoken to... which is a large number by the way. However time and time again I see huge AGENT FIRST scripting mistakes. Right now the largest one I see is asking the lead if they have an agent helping them too soon in the conversation. Far too many people do this right off the bat, as the first or second question they ask. This question has no benefit to the client and has nothing to do with their purchasing or selling a home. Yes most boards require the agent to ask this ...

before offering to provide services, but not before we find out some information about the lead.

This is one example, but the problem is rampant. When you have a script written out, examine it and put yourself in the mind of different buyers and ask yourself, could this question offend me, is this the very best way to ask this, do I feel like the agent cares about me or themselves? Do I feel extra or unwanted pressure from this question?

Scripts are our first impression with people most of the time, make them feel like we care about them first and ourselves second and they will want to have more to do with us.

These five truisms have very little to do with the actual words that are said. I have personally used at least four different "other's Scripts" and 1 of my own that I have altered many times. My script was built from the best parts of other scripts and my own testing and improvements over the years, they have worked for people I have trained and for me over the years. However I saw many other people try to do this exact same script with little to no success. It all came down to understanding and respecting the truisms.

TIP: Leaving messages waste time – rarely do leads call you back so once a voice mail is reached, hang up and move on to the next call. Avoiding messages can lead to 30-50 more dials in a 6-hour shift that can lead to numerous more appointments.

How to Build a Script

I fear not the man who has practiced 10,000 kicks once, but I fear the man who has practiced one kick 10,000 times
~~~ Bruce Lee

A long time ago, I made a decision not only to share my scripts but teach people how to build a script as well. Frankly I believe 100% that it is unimportant which option you choose. If you are looking to build your own script, start from what you know works and improve from there. Know that there are many parts to a script. It is not one simple all encompassing thing. That is a script book. You minimally need an Introduction Script, an Offer Script and Objection Handling Scripts. Let me tell you what I look for in each. Remember, each part of a script has it's own purpose, but most of us tend to place a much larger overall purpose on each individual part. The script as a whole has the job of booking appointments, and each section builds towards that ultimate goal. Don't try to do too much in any one step or the script will fall apart.

Introduction Script

This should deal with how to quickly introduce the salesperson and why they are calling. It should not waste time on pleasantries and should immediately use the Philosophy of Counteraction to get the lead in the mood to answer questions. The Intro script should have 4-7 questions that help the salesperson determine timing and motivation, and simply put, answer the question "do I want to work with this person?" That is the sole purpose for this portion of the script.

Tip: Do not ask AGENT-CENTRIC questions until the end (e.g. Do you have an agent you are working with?)

Offer Script

This part of the script is for letting the lead know what service I am offering to provide, find out if they want it and the close the lead for an appointment. This offer should be full of value and make you sound different and better than your competition. This is the most important script in your arsenal. The better this script is, and the better it is delivered, the more appointments you will get and the fewer objections you will face.

The offer is best used split in two parts, first getting the client to state that they want what we have, followed by telling them what they need to do in order to get it. This way we know that should they object, they are objecting to the information or the requirements. This is very important for improving my Objection Handle techniques.

Objection Handles

Objections are simply excuses a client gives us to not do business in the manner we wish it done... unless the excuse is legitimate. A legitimate problem cannot be overcome, excuses are flimsy and with a quality logical approach seem to vanish in the air.

This is the true make or break portion of a script. Can you handle what excuses a client may say to you? In real estate there are approximately 13 objections a buyer might use to avoid an appointment or the information you can provide, and about 8 objections sellers might use. Of these only 3 buyer objections and 2 seller objections make up over 90% of the excuses you will face and honestly one is the same objection in both situation. The biggest problem is that there are more than 100 ways to say each objection, and the client might combine these objections together to make a super objection too.

The objections are common, and the same worldwide, it is easy to sit down and come up with ways to handle them, write them down and learn them. "I'm too Busy, Can't I just tell you now, I need to check with my spouse, What is your commission rate?" Probably the very best part to creating the objection handles is the immense power it gives to a Salesperson. Knowing that you have a logical response to each and every scenario that a lead can throw at you creates a level of calm confidence that, not only allows you to book more appointments, but make more calls as well. It is a double win for the agent that takes the time to prepare.

So how do we create an objection handle? You need to follow a simple system called LISA.

Step One: Listen and Agree with the client
Step Two: Identify and highlight the problem
Step Three: Solve the Problem
Step Four: Ask for the Appointment

Step one and four are the most commonly missed steps in the process. Each step is equally important. The first step sets the tone, one of co-operation not adversarial. Step two allows us to be on the same page and see the problem that needs to be solved. Step three provides a logical solution to the problem and step four closes the topic as an objection and returns us to the real problem, the appointment. This is a very important part of the process so I have included an article I wrote about Objection Handling that will expand on this topic and help you create great objection handling techniques.

If you can follow this pattern when writing or responding to an objection, you will discover its legitimacy. This is the true job of objection handling, to determine if the excuse is real or not ... that is all. We can expose excuse after excuse, but this alone will not book an appointment. Because of this fact, I will only ever expose two excuses in any given call before scheduling a follow up call instead of an appointment to meet face to face. Too many objections is a sign the client is being difficult, this is either because they are a difficult person (the vast minority) or because I am talking to them too early in their process for them to feel comfortable in meeting with a sales representative. So I need to plan a call at a future date in order to provide the level of service the client wants and leave the client with a positive feeling about my company and me.

How to Learn a Script

"Practice is where you BECOME the very best in the world, Game day is when you prove it."
~~ Andy Herrington

Learning a script WORD for WORD is a major struggle for many people. I wish I could say that there is one simple way to do it, however there just isn't. It is a very personal thing. I will however give you a bunch of different ideas on how to tackle scripting and learn it as best you can.

The biggest key to any of these ideas is repetition. Doing it over and over again until it is ingrained in your brain. The idea is to get to the point where the words are simply a part of you and you do not need to think at all as they flow out from you.

Ways to Learn a Script:

Mental Repetition: this is where you read the words over and over in your mind. You think the words and test yourself by removing the visual words. This is one of the most commonly used and most difficult ways to learn a script; I honestly do not recommend it at all.

Vocal Repetition: This is where you read the words out loud over and over. You speak the words and test yourself by removing the visual words. The most common mistake in this format is trying to learn the entire piece at once, rather than breaking it up sentence-by-sentence and learning each sentence by itself. Imagine a paragraph with 4 sentences. The best way to use Vocal repetition is to say only sentence 1 over and over again until you can do it without the paper in hand. Then move to sentence 2 and learn it the same then combine sentence 1 & 2... This is a very good way to learn a script.

Written Repetition: For many people writing out the script over and over, first copying word for word from another piece of paper then from memory, and checking it against a good copy. The step of checking it tends to be missed which has the side effect of ingraining mistakes instead of correcting them. This is usually a great tool as an add on to another technique, but for certain people can work well all on its own.

Pneumatic Devices: Just like in grade school, BEDMAS for math, or ROYGBIV for the colours of the rainbow, pneumatic devices can help you out. They can be exactly like that remembering things in the right order by letters putting things into a 'sing-song' format, or more likely for adults by using actions. The brain is amazing, if you say the same thing over and over and associate it with an action, like touching your thumb and index finger, the two will become linked. This means that you can then touch your thumb and index finger together and that action will help you remember the words to say. Don't believe me, try it you will be amazed.

Role-Play: Practicing real life scenarios with another person is by far the best way to learn a script. The competition aspect if you are both learning is also helpful. However make sure you have someone there that is listening for and being critical of the mistakes.

Self – Evaluation: As you role-play, or even get on the phones, self-evaluation is a major key in learning your scripts and keeping your scripts accurate over time. Take a moment after any role-play, call or practice session and evaluate what you did right and wrong. What you need to focus on improving and what you used to do and no longer are doing. This time is where you truly improve.

Lastly I want to give you an idea on how long it takes to learn a script. For most people who are working at it everyday, and spending time incorporating numerous tactics to learn the script, it should take 2-4 weeks to be able to comfortably say the script from memory. However, It will then take 2-4 months to ingrain that script into your brain so you do not have to think about what you are saying as you say it. This is where you have achieved true WORD for WORD knowledge of the script. So give yourself enough time to learn the script and use it.

ARTICLE: THE ART OF HANDLING OBJECTIONS
By: Andy Herrington

First things first let me define the word objection for you so we are on the same page. Objections are _direct statements_ from a client, customer or lead that are being used as an _excuse_ not to do something with or get something from you the realtor. This 'something' could be signing a contract, making a legitimate offer, booking an appointment or simply obtaining information. People object to just about anything and everything at one time or another.

Now that we know what an objection is, let me take a moment to say what they are not. Objections are not legitimate reasons the person cannot do or get something. Sometimes objections and legitimate reasons look very similar so one needs to treat them the same until they know the excuse is real. How do you know the excuse is real? Well when you handle the excuse with quality and logic the objector continues with the same excuse. This means even though there is a logical solution it just will not solve their issue.

So what then is the best way to handle an objection? Well, it involves a Four-step process. "LISA" – Listen, Identify, Solve and Ask.

- Step one   – Listen and Agree with The Person.
- Step two   – Identify and point out the problem with the persons thinking,
- Step three – Solve the person's problem.
- Step four   – Ask for closure.

I will go into more detail on each so that as you face objections in your future dealings you will know how to follow this approach.

Step one – Listen and agree with the person

This is a vital step in ensuring that you are handling the correct objection and creating an environment where the objector will listen to you as you continue to handle their problem. This is essential so we are not immediately perceived as arguing with the objector. We want to be viewed as someone who is on the same page as the Objector. We will accomplish nothing and not get the outcome we desire if we skip this step.

We will listen to what they are saying and identify the issue, possibly even clarify with a question to ensure we are on the same page. Remember the same objection can be said in a huge multitude of ways. Our next actions will be to agree with them in part. (Eg. "I'm Too Busy" – respond with, As a busy person yourself, you are well aware of ...) then continue on in the process. We do not argue that what they are saying is wrong, we agree with them (in part) even if they are wrong. We do this so that the person will listen to the remainder of the objection handle.

Step two – Identify and point out the problem with the persons thinking

Once we are seen as listening to them and agreeing with them we begin to turn the conversation to our agenda. We need to use the Objection to point out the flaw in the objector's issue. We need to show that the objection is actually part of the problem, not that which they are objecting too. (e.g. ... the sheer volume of listings and information that is out there today and the time that it would take someone to navigate to the best information is truly daunting ...)

Step three – Solve the person's problem.

Now we need to show how what they are objecting to is the solution to the new problem we created together. We need to provide them a better way that when viewed logically will solve the clients issue and make the clients life easier and better. (e.g. ...However what I am going to do will save you hours of time by making sure you are exposed to the very best information as quickly as possible....)

Step four – Ask for Closure.

This is easily the most skipped step in the process. Once we have identified the problem, showed the real issue and the solution to the problem, we must act confident as we now know the problem is solved. Using that confidence we must return to the original offer (of service, contracts, offer...) and ask again for what the client needs to do. (e.g. ... it only takes 10-15 min now when is the best time for us to meet? {provide options of times I. E. Monday or Tuesday})

Conclusion

Now hopefully, since we have solved their "problem" they will now be closer to or in fact ready to book an appointment or write the offer, or do the action to which they were objecting to in the first place, once again if they repeat the same objection that is a sign that either we did a poor job providing the logical solution or the Objection is a Legitimate excuse.

It is also at this time where they might throw out a new objection. This is a sign they are still trying to avoid the necessary action we know is best for them. Handle this second objection using the same "LISA" technique. Provide a nice and firm approach and do your best to calm their worries. However, if they should come up with a third different objection, this is a sign that the client is being difficult and truly at this moment you are not going to be able to turn their mind without causing damage to your own reputation in their minds. At this point break off the conversation in a friendly way and let the client know you will revisit the subject in the future. Then go about your day, talk to more people and handle their objections, and more people and more objections.

Once you become a real wiz at this method you will be far more confident to talk to more people at anytime and in anyplace. You will see a marked improvement in your conversion skills that will in turn affect the bottom line. You will make more contacts with people because you know that you can handle anything they plan to throw at you. You know that if you don't help them know you can the next time you speak to them. You will frankly make more money and get more respect.

CHAPTER TEN

How the Right words help you sell

The difference between the almost right word & the right word is the difference between the lightning bug and the lightning. ~~~ Mark Twain

In Sales the difference between the right word and another word can be the difference between getting paid and getting welfare. Using certain words can send a message that you do not wish to send. The psychological effects of words, that we as sales people use regularly, on the general public is amazing. They can drastically affect our ability to book appointments or sign contracts.

We all know that the words we use when marketing have a huge effect on the number of leads that are returned to us, however, very few take this concept into the sales process at all.

Many of the words that salespeople use have very harsh and frankly scary intonations associated with them. Using the wrong words can leave the client with the impression that we are pushy, where the same message could be portrayed as helpful and insightful when using the right words. I have built a table to provide you with the words or statements to avoid. In most instances we have what words to say in their place, however there are certain words and statements that simply must be avoided all together and others that should be added to your repertoire.

Avoid These	Try these
With sellers – Home / With buyers -House	With buyers – Home / With sellers -House
What do you want …	What do you need …
Let me tell you about what we do…	Let me tell you how what we do, can Benefit you…
Buy	Own
Customer / Lead	Client
Cost / Commission	Investment / Fee
I	We / our
Would you like to make an Offer?	Would you like to see what kind of a good deal we could get on this? At what price would you be willing to take this home?
No Problem	I will get you the answer you need
We have a system…	This would work for you…
Everyone else is doing this…	Soon everyone will do this…
Who is the decision maker	Who else is influencing your decisions?
Do you have any questions?	What questions can I answer for you?
Keep us in mind for the future…	When would be a good time for me to follow up?

I think so... / I believe so...	Definitely, Absolutely
Sign	Authorize
Contract	Agreement or Paperwork
You need to ..., You have to ...	Our options are ...
Add to your Vocabulary	I understand you ...
Add to your Vocabulary	I would be happy to assist you...
Add to your Vocabulary	I suggest... / I recommend...
Add to your Vocabulary	What we can do right now...
Add to your Vocabulary	I am sorry, let me make that up to you by ....
Add to your Vocabulary	I never find it a waste of my time to help people...
Add to your Vocabulary	My job is to help people make Quality Real Estate decisions, even if that decision is to NOT buy a home.
Obviously	Remove from your vocabulary
Just	Remove from your vocabulary
Basically	Remove from your vocabulary
To be honest with you / To tell you the truth	Remove from your vocabulary

Trust me	Remove from your vocabulary
Always / Never	Remove from your vocabulary
This is perfect for everyone	Remove from your vocabulary

Now these words are a great list, it is by no means complete, nor is it correct 100% of the time. It is a good list to demonstrate the mentality that we need to possess when we are in a sales situation. Do we want to be perceived as a salesperson (Used car or otherwise), or as a trusted consultant? The real point of this chapter is really just to get us to think more about what we say and how we say it. It truly can make the difference between becoming a millionaire or not.

TIP: Call when they are home – The best time for calling is evening, weekends and holidays, a great phone specialist calls during Stat Holidays the rewards are very high!

TIP: Dress for success – You may think you are just on the phone and no one can see you but, you will portray a more professional front if you are dressed properly as well.

CHAPTER ELEVEN
Setting up your Workspace

The Studio, a room to which the artist consigns him/herself for life, is naturally important, not only as a workplace, but as a source of inspiration.
~~~ Grace Glueck

This may seem a bit strange, but there are a whole slew of benefits that can come from having a well set up workplace. It will allow you to become more fluent on the phone in any and all situations.

Personally I find windows to be overrated, but for many people they are a necessity, you will need to know what is better for yourself. However, I believe nice pictures or paintings can provide just as much scenery with far less distraction.

For the Aesthetic minded of us out there, I believe painting an office in a pleasing colour provides for better longer lasting energy. The stark white or off-white workplaces that I regularly see are not conducive to a calm and relaxed phone specialist. Personally I like rich beiges, greens and blues. But I would choose a colour the actual person working in the office likes. This may seem like a silly expense to paint, but the fresh environment will pay you back for sure.

Famous quotes and pictures of goals are important. Quotes that are the persons favourite, or ones that reflex what the team is striving to accomplish. Not all quotes should be "work harder" quotes, some should be funny, and uplifting quotes others can be focus and driven based quotes. These can be fancy posters or simply print outs on paper. Pictures of Goals are personal and should be chosen and placed by the phone specialist.

Tracking needs to have a central location and be always present while not over powering the room. It should not be placed where the specialist must look at it all the time, but be handy for when they need to see it. It should include a tally board with Appointments booked, Appointments Met, No Shows and Contracts signed for each agent who is having appointments booked for them. This should be out in the open for all to see. There should be a monthly calendar used as an Appointments booked per day tally board. All phone specialists should be putting the number of appointments booked on a day on the same calendar. Lastly and this should be the smallest board, there should be a Deal Tracker for transactions completed that the specialists booked the original appointment.

Most important is the personal workspace for the Phone specialist. They need a desk, phone, headset, pens and paper and a computer. They should have their own space that they use every time they call. Some of the essentials in setting up this space is a Large Print version of the Script book, which should be taped to the wall all around the phone. They can be in any order that the specialist deems appropriate, but for me I had my phone in a central location on the desk just to the right of my computer. Right above it on the wall was my Buyer Offer, and above that the seller offer and at the top of that the introduction script with my 'five questions'. To the left I had my buyer objections, to the right was first a Mirror, then the Seller Objections, and the objections were in order from most common to least common.

This allowed me to at the drop of a hat look on my wall and ensure that I would be word for word perfect when delivering my scripts, even if I forgot a part or stumbled. Truthfully I rarely used the scripts up there during a call, but they were instrumental in my post call evaluation, and were a saviour now and then when I would have a brain fart.

The mirror was a good tool for reminding me about posture, smiling and my energy level. It helps to centre you and ensure the proper attitude while dialing the phone.

Lastly I only mentioned in passing the headset, I believe 100% that a headset is an imperative tool for the phone specialist. It reduces fatigue, and allows the freedom of movement for note taking and using a computer. Not providing a headset will reduce the phone specialists dial rate by 33-45%, which far outweighs any costs attached to this piece of equipment. Personally I have used both Corded and wireless headsets. Wireless allows for much more freedom, even if there is a long cord on the corded one. That said if costs are an issue, the main benefits lie in the headset itself not its cord or lack there of.

TIP: CRM is your communication tool – Use the CRM to pass notes and check up on appointments it will save you time allowing you to make more dials.

CHAPTER TWELVE
Bonus Articles

ARTICLE: WHAT CAN A REALTOR LEARN FROM STEVE JOBS?

By: Andy Herrington

One of the greatest minds, greatest salesmen and possibly worst people just recently left this world. He left behind a legacy that will be hard to duplicate. But he also left behind some very good lessons for us. If we want to look at them and instill them into our own businesses we can see incredible results. But what can a Real Estate Salesperson learn from a CEO of a multibillion-dollar computer company?

I have 3 major lessons I'd like to share with you that I think everyone could learn and implement and see tangible results in a short period of time.

Number 1: Earth Stopping Showmanship

If nothing else Steve Jobs is a showman. He understood the importance of being a spectacle. Apple Inc. became a worldwide phenomenon in 1984. It was a commercial that did it. Not the computers or the innovations but a lone Super Bowl Ad that had amazing imagery and shockingly long staying power. The ad really needs no introduction and if you don't know what I am speaking of go to Google and type Apple 1984 and you will find the video. It is an ad that has won honour after honour in the Advertising world. It got a continent talking about Apple Inc. and it was only telecast ONCE!

What Steve Jobs then did was follow that up with an amazing stage presentation of the product the commercial eluded too, and follower that up with another great Ad campaign "Think Different". While the lessons of 1984 and the Macintosh unveiling are important, it is the campaign "Think Different" that I think Realtors need to pay most attention to.

Real estate agents over the years have fallen in a trap. They have become a massive lump of "Realtors" and hardly any stand out from the crowd. This is where you can find an advantage. Think Different than your competition; figure out how you can be seen amongst the massive lump and be seen as Different, because only then can you ever be seen as better. Then continue the path and provide different and better service and results. If you are different you will be talked about and your reputation will grow.

Become the showman some who steps out from the crowd.

Number 2: Fanatical Attention to Detail

Apple inc. is known the world over for their sleek and stylish design. They are known for having amazing innovations that no one else could think of. They are known for taking care of the little things, the details.

Real estate salespeople should be no different. Ensure that the details are covered, the smallest ones to the biggest ones. Don't have spelling mistakes, or an offer that has no flow to it. Have a social media presence, and a PowerPoint presentation. Show your clients that you are a professional and that you take every aspect of your job seriously. They will feel better, safer and less stressed throughout the process, and remember at the end of the day, after all is said and done, your clients do not remember the words that you say, they do not remember the things that you do or the Ad's that you wrote, but they will remember HOW YOU MADE THEM FEEL. Attention to detail is the single best way to make a hugely positive impression on people, and if you make a positive impression you will be talked about and your reputation will grow.

Number 3: Laser-like Focus

Steve Jobs took this lesson to a whole other level, and frankly went too far ostracizing most of the people in his life. But there is still a huge lesson to learn. Jobs took Apple down a path of Focus. They wanted to become the premier Computer in the world. They would have 4 products (in the beginning) Home and professional style Laptops and Desktops. They would control everything and they would be focused on innovation and the fine details making the experience the best for the end user.

Everything they did as the company grew continued to have this laser-like focus. They focused on a maximum of 3 products at a time, improving and perfecting them all. They didn't worry about making a zillion different varieties of each computer, but one or two. They targeted and captured the top 10% of the computer marketplace, the people who were willing to pay more for better equipment. And they focused on them. This focus has after a long time slowly made the Apple a mainstream product known for its innovation and superior function. They can sell their product for more money and have ridiculous loyalty from their focus group.

Realtors can do the same. Focus your attention on the people you want to work with, stop trying to please everyone and do everything. Focus on improving one aspect of your business at a time and try to capture a specific audience with your unique selling proposition. Focus on small incremental changes over a period of time, rather than looking for unimaginable results by tomorrow. We tend to jump at everything we see and don't give anything the focus it deserves. This leads to a jumbled mess and frankly things start to fall through the cracks.

Focus your efforts and soon enough you will be known for that focus. You will be able to provide service to that focus group that no one else can match. You will be seen as providing a service beyond what your competition does. If you are known for service beyond your competition, you will be talked about and your reputation will grow.

If we look at Apple computers and Steve Jobs we see an outline for success. But it wasn't simply the innovations and well built computers, but the philosophies behind the company that made it the success it is today. What are the philosophies behind your business? Can you find the focus, the attention to detail and the Showmanship in your business?

ARTICLE: 6 STEPS TO CHANGING PERCEPTION!
By: Andy Herrington

As we begin the New Year, every small business owner needs to ask him or herself one simple question. "What do people think about my Business or me?" The answer is the reality that we live in. Our business' success or failure is tied to the public's perception of the business and us.

Remember that as Dr. Richard Bandler says, "There is no reality, only perceived reality." This means that whatever our clientele thinks of our business or us is in fact the reality of what our business is.

Over the years, I created an exercise I could do at the beginning of every year to be in control of the perception of my business. Well, in control at least as much as one can have over these things.

What I came up with was a focused approach to creating the reputation I wanted. I needed to define the business and myself, as I wanted them to be perceived, and then keep that mindset throughout the year. I had pages and pages of ways I wanted my Business and me to be perceived. I realized that, the truth was, "whatever people thought of the owner, was the reality of what they thought of the business. As a small business owner we are forever linked."

This was a step forward, now I could cut my list of perceptions down to just how I wanted people to perceive me. I asked myself, what was the best way to accomplish my desires of perfect perception? The answer was "a consistent focused personalized approach can direct my actions into the desired outcome I had designed."

I cannot create pages and pages of perceptions in other people. However if I focus I can create 1 of 3 perceptions on a regular basis. I have taken a lot of time and effort looking at this number. Frankly I want it to be 5 or even 10, but I know that the key number is three. I can project a consistent perception on one of three fronts at all times, all year, with all people.

So what I do each year is sit down and decide "What 3 words or phrases do I want people to associate with me?" In order to come up with those perceptions, I follow these 7 steps:

1. Start with a strict ten-minute session writing down all the ideas regarding the perception of your business. NO FILTER ALLOWED! Even write silly thoughts.

2. Then group the similar words together and make "groups of ideas", and cross out the useless ones.
3. In each group choose the very best word or phrase.
4. Review all solo ideas and the best of each group. Choose only your TOP THREE.
5. Write the Top Three on their own piece of paper. Try to take up the majority of the paper with these three words.
6. Post these words everywhere you spend some time during the day. Near computers, Phones, Bathroom, Shower, Car...
7. As you make decisions and communicate throughout the day, ask yourself "will this person perceive this as (one of my three words)? If the answer is no, make a better decision, or communicate it in a better way.

We can always portray 1 of 3 things in all of our dealings with the public. The vital understanding we must have is that "to be perceived in a specific state, we need the other person to view us in their <u>own mind, as their own definition</u> of that specific state." Keeping this in mind, decide WHAT to project, consciously CHOOSE to project the image in the way that each specific client needs, and do it on a CONSISTENT basis for an extended period of time.

When you follow this approach you will improve the reputation and the reality that surrounds your business, and drastically increase your bottom line. Here's to getting and even better start to another great year!

ARTICLE: THE MAGIC OF MASTERY
By: Andy Herrington

Malcolm Gladwell's book, "Outliers", brought the concept of the 10,000 hour rule into the mainstream consciousness – the theory says that it takes a person 10,000 hours of "deliberate practice" to become a Master in any given field. So if it is this simple, take a little over 1 year, 416.67 days to be more precise (double this if you want to sleep at all) to become a master, why are so few Realtors truly "masterful" in real estate?

In every area you will have a handful of masters in different pieces of Real Estate. Buyers, Sellers, Marketing, Social Media, Farming, the list goes on. They are the innovators and trail blazers. They see what will happen, and are seemingly always in the right place at the right time. The first thing I notice is that very few are masters in multiple areas. I began to study this and have found that the 10,000 hours is important, however the phrase "deliberate practice" is a little too simplified for most people. The three main keys to becoming a master, is

1.   Deliberate practice
2.   Practical application
3.   Focus

Most people have time for only one piece of the puzzle; practical application, actually doing the business. They do not have time for daily specific practice and cannot afford to focus on one area of Real Estate.

Practice is about being perfect, Practical application rarely ever is. Practice is imperative because it finds the errors in our ways, and refines our systems into more powerful tools. The very best of the best ... the Masters, specifically schedule and set aside time to practice, learn and grow in their focused area of expertise. They seek out new ways and refine their own specialty so they are never behind the times. They understand and place a high value on improvement, which allows them to never be stagnant in their business.

The last element is truly the hardest because there are so many distractions for the Realtor these days. For many that do find the time to practice and practically apply what they practice they lack the blind focus, and end up trying a little of everything and becoming a jack-of-all-trades but a master of none. Look at sports, the greatest players do one or two things better than everyone else. Elite Players are faster, or harder, or more accurate or better strategists... but rarely is any one player the best in all of those categories. In hockey the hardest shooter is not the most accurate and in baseball the home run hitter is never the hardest throwing pitcher. At the same time, in all sports there are many players that are "all around players", but they are never the superstars. The Real Estate industry works the same way; it is too vast to become a master in many different areas. Focus is needed to truly carve out your place and become the Superstar you know you are.

Now looking at these 10,000 hours we can see it is a whole lot harder to achieve widespread mastery. In the average work year there is 3744 hours of work a year. Most of us do not spend 30min a week in "practice" mode. That is 26 hours a year – at this rate it will take a person 384.61 years to become a master. Next we can add the practical application, this even when we are working 10 hour days 6 days a week will at most count for 14focused hours a week. The rest of our time is spent on the other tasks of being a Real Estate Agent. We now only need 13.74 years to become a master in one aspect of Real Estate. The real issue is that you cannot focus on multiple areas at a time and truly expect to ever reach mastery. So if you are in the business for 30 years, you likely can become an expert in TWO categories. This also assumes that you can focus for 14 years on a specific area at a time. Mastery is simple, but it is not easy.

We all know the experts in our areas. "The Farmer", "The Lister", "The Marketer", "The Buyers Agent" and we know in our hearts that we are better at this or that than they are, we are smarter, and we work harder.... We all wonder how they accomplished so much with what appears to be so little. It is their ability to Focus, their dedication to specific deliberate Practice and their consistent Practical Application of the very best systems that creates their Superstar status.

So if you want to be the Superstar you wish to be, find your desired expertise, and focus on it, work hard day after day and do not lose sight. Do not get distracted. Do not quit. And over time you will become that hugely successful Realtor in your area that no one can understand why they get so much business with what appears to be so little.

ARTICLE: 27 DAYS TO VICTORY
By: Andy Herrington

This is a process that guarantees upon successful completion to have obtained complete victory. The process is 27 days long. The first thing to know is that the results will not occur on day 1, 2 or even 26. They will occur on day 27, not before. So the very first thing you have to do is to fully commit to 27 days IN A ROW, for this to work. If you skip a day, or even only do only 90% of a day, the results will not occur and you must start over. The process is simple, but not easy, it is hard work and takes a lot of focus, but the rewards are immense.

Once you have committed, the next thing to do is decide what ONE THING you want. The one thing you can focus on and want to have at the end of 27 days. This can be anything, more money, lose weight, more appointments, more leads... any single thing you may desire. However it must be exceedingly important to you, very specific, and something you wholeheartedly believe that there is nothing that could possibly get in your way

114

of accomplishing that you do not have the skills and imagination to overcome.

Take that one thing and write it down (in the present tense) on 27 cards (i.e. "I have earned 50,000 dollars this month" or "I weigh 150lbs"), and date every card. This card should be big enough to hold the goal, and small enough to be carried around with you all day. On the back of the card I want you to place 15 empty boxes or circles, evenly spaced. Take the stack of cards and place them all on your dresser, bathroom counter, or a similar spot you use every day when you wake up and before you go to bed.

The first activity in the process is that every morning you wake up, and take your card for the day. You will read the card aloud once and to yourself once. Flip the card over and make a check in one of the boxes. Then think about (even write down separately) what you need to do that day (specific tasks) to help make the statement a reality. Then get on with your day. Carry the card with you all day. Look at the card as many times as you can every day, read it aloud and to yourself each time. Believe the statement wholeheartedly. Anytime you doubt yourself, read the card. Anytime you get sidetracked, read the card. When you have a free moment in the day read the card. After reading the card, make a mark, and then get back to work. At the end of the day take the card out and read it again, flip it over make one last mark and start a new pile where the cards are kept for "used cards". Do this day after day for 27 straight days.

The rest of the day, keep these words in your mind – "DO MORE THAN YOU HAVE TO." Do more than the bare minimum; in fact go above and beyond in every activity, in every interaction, on every task and in every way. {I like to call it – "Doing your very best... Blindfolded." For those that do not know what I mean by this, send a quick email and I will forward you a great video that will outline it perfectly (andy@andyherrington.com)}. As you move through the day with every task being done at a superior level, you will create a level of service that brings with it an immense satisfaction. As obstacles come, you will face them head on, and use your positive mindset and imagination to solve them and overcome them never taking your eyes of the prize.

Worries and Doubts must be fully removed or the process will not work. Knowing where you are going is far more important than knowing exactly how the entire journey is going to happen. When we are in the moment, calm, focused and positive at what the outcome will be; we are able to overcome anything, create our desired outcome and be victorious.

ABOUT THE AUTHOR

Andy Herrington is a Canadian Real Estate Salesperson, International Author, High Energy Speaker and Real Estate Business Coach. He was a part of 3 of the Top Real Estate Sales Teams on Canada's Largest Real Estate Board. For 6 Years, he was an active member and manager for the different team's Inside Sales Teams as a Phone Specialist. During this stretch these teams averaged over 350 sales a year, and completed in excess of 2100 deals. In 4 of those 6 years the team he was on ranked #1 on Canada's Largest Real estate Board, the Toronto Real Estate Board for Units sold or Volume of sales.

Andy went on to be the Director of Coaching and a Master Coach for the first "Team Specific" training company Dan Plowman Team Systems. He stayed there for 4 years, before branching off on his own to develop and build Powerhouse Coaching. This allowed Andy the freedom to use all of the knowledge from all of the teams he has been a part of either as Team Member or as a Master Coach.

Over the years Andy has coached 7 of the Top 15 Producers in the Toronto Real Estate Board, as well as the Top Producer in 5 other Canadian Real Estate Boards. Andy has helped Real Estate Salespeople all across Canada strive to do better and make the Industry a more professional place.

Andy has had numerous articles published internationally as well as in Canada, most notably in SOLD

Magazine and REM magazine. He runs a blog @ andyherrington.com and can be seen at speaking engagements across North America.

Lastly To inquire about having Andy speak to your team or brokerage or have Andy as your coach, or your teams coach contact him directly @ andy@andyherrington.com, you will not be disappointed.

Made in the USA
Charleston, SC
06 September 2013